C

Dinosaur World

Emily Bone

Illustrated by Lee Cosgrove

Designed by Zoe Wray

Dinosaurs consultant. Dr. Darren Naish,
University of Southampton
Reading consultant: Alison Kelly

Contents

World of dinosaurs

Millions of years ago, animals called dinosaurs lived all over the world.

Maiasaura roamed around in big herds.

They charged at other dinosaurs to scare them away.

Different dinosaurs

A dinosaur was a type of reptile,
like lizards and crocodiles. There were
lots of different kinds.

Brachiosaurus were huge.
They had long necks
and scaly skin.

Citipati ran around on two legs.
They were covered in feathers.

4

Pinacosaurus had rows of sharp spines on its back and tail.

Tarbosaurus had big, sharp teeth and claws for attacking other dinosaurs.

Big and small

Some dinosaurs were much, much bigger than animals alive today. Others were very small.

Ankylosaurus was almost as long as a bus.

Argentinosaurus

Argentinosaurus
was one of the
biggest dinosaurs.
It was heavier than
16 elephants.

A Microraptor
was smaller
than a chicken.

Around the world

The world was much hotter when the dinosaurs were alive. There were lots of scorching, dry deserts.

Gobivenator ran across the hot sand.

Protoceratops ate any plants that grew.

Some places had wide, deep rivers flowing through them.

Big crocodiles lived there. They hunted dinosaurs who came to drink.

Most of the world was covered in thick, steamy forests.

Plant eaters

Many dinosaurs roamed around the forests looking for plants to eat.

Stegosaurus had a sharp mouth, like a beak. It bit through plant stalks.

Diplodocus had a long neck to
reach leaves high up in tall trees.

It could stretch out
to grab plants too.

Super hunters

Some dinosaurs ate meat. They had big teeth and sharp claws to hunt other animals.

Velociraptor ran very fast to grab its prey.

It used its deadly claws to pin the animal to the ground.

Baryonyx hunted for fish
in rivers and swamps.

It had a big claw on its hand
to spear fish out of the water.

King of the dinosaurs

Tyrannosaurus rex was one of the biggest, fiercest dinosaurs.

Its huge mouth was full of razor-sharp teeth.

Tyrannosaurus were skilled hunters.

A Tyrannosaurus charged
at the dinosaur it
wanted to eat.

Then it grabbed the dinosaur
in its powerful mouth.

Keeping safe

The dinosaur world could be a dangerous place. Dinosaurs had different ways of protecting themselves.

Ankylosaurus had a bony club on the end of its tail to hit attacking dinosaurs.

Triceratops had a tough frill to stop other dinosaurs from biting its neck.

It could stab dinosaurs with its sharp horns to make them go away.

Dinosaur babies

Baby dinosaurs hatched out of eggs.

A mother Citipati scraped out a hollow in the ground to make a nest.

She laid lots of eggs in the nest.

The parents took turns sitting on the eggs to keep them warm.

Little baby Citipati hatched out of the eggs.

In the air

Other creatures lived at the same time as the dinosaurs. Pterosaurs were reptiles with big, flapping wings.

Pterodactylus flew after insects.

Rhamphorhynchus swooped down to catch fish.

Hatzegopteryx was a giant pterosaur, as tall as a giraffe.

It mostly walked around on land, hunting small dinosaurs.

Under the sea

All kinds of fearsome creatures lived under the sea too.

Tylosaurus were huge reptiles that hunted sharks.

Ammonites were sea creatures with shells.

Mosasaurus
dived down
after giant
squid.

Where have they gone?

There were dinosaurs on Earth for millions of years but then they died out.

Many scientists think that a massive rock from space crashed into the Earth.

Clouds of dust filled the sky. It became cold and dark and many plants died.

Plant-eating dinosaurs had nothing to eat. Slowly they died out.

Meat-eating dinosaurs had nothing to eat either. They died out too.

How do we know?

We know dinosaurs existed because we've found their bones under the ground.

Over millions of years, the bones became buried and slowly turned to stone. Now they're called fossils.

This is the fossil of a Triceratops.

When scientists find dinosaur fossils,
they carefully dig them up.

They take the fossils back to a laboratory
and clean off any dirt.

Putting them together

Once scientists have cleaned up the fossils of dinosaur bones, they have to fit them back together.

These are the bones of an Argentinosaurus.

Psittacosaurus

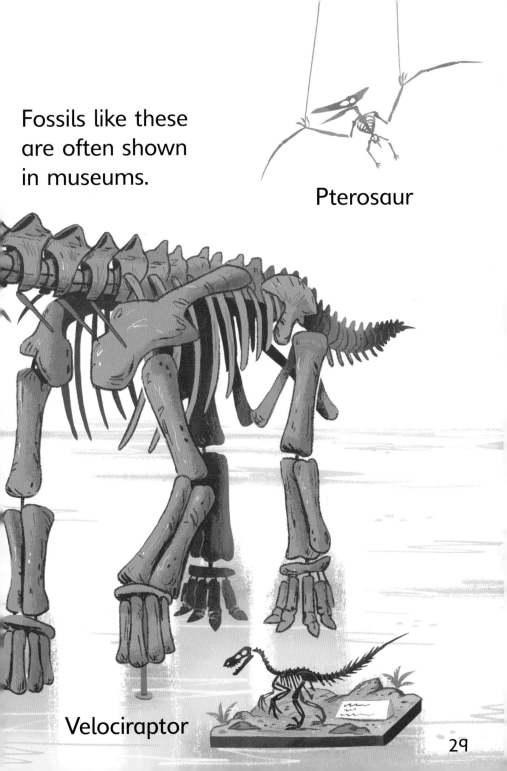

Fossils like these are often shown in museums.

Pterosaur

Velociraptor

Glossary

Here are some of the words in this book you might not know. This page tells you what they mean.

 herd - a group of animals that live together.

 scales - hard discs that covered the skin of some dinosaurs.

 claw - a sharp spike on the finger or toe of meat-eating dinosaurs.

 prey - animals hunted by other animals for food.

 frill - a bony piece of skin that protected the neck of a triceratops.

 pterosaur - a flying reptile alive at the same time as the dinosaurs.

 fossils - the bones of a dinosaur that have turned to stone.

Usborne Quicklinks

Would you like to discover lots more about dinosaurs?
Visit Usborne Quicklinks for links to exciting websites
with video clips, amazing facts and fun things to make
and do. You will also find a pronunciation guide to
hear how to say all the dinosaur names in this book.

Go to **usborne.com/Quicklinks** and type in the
keywords "**beginners dinosaur world**".
Make sure you ask a grown-up before going online.

Notes for grown-ups

Please read the internet safety guidelines at the Usborne
Quicklinks website with your child. Children should be
supervised online. The websites are regularly reviewed and the
links at Usborne Quicklinks are updated. However, Usborne
Publishing is not responsible and does not accept liability for
the content or availability of any website other than its own.

Some dinosaur footprints
have turned into fossils too.
These are the footprints
of Acrocanthosaurus.

Index

Acknowledgements

Managing Designer: Zoe Wray

Additional design by Tabitha Blore

Digital retouching by John Russell